B is for Blue Crab

A Maryland Alphabet

Written by Shirley C. Menendez and Illustrated by Laura Stutzman

Laura Stutzman would like to thank: Braxton Strueber; Asa McCain; The Treaty of Paris Restaurant; Josey, Matt & Brevin Redinger; Fowl Boy the dog; Historic St. Mary's City & Joseph Greeley; Connie Reams; Fort Frederick and its reenactors; the reenactors at Antietam National Battlefield; The Maryland Renaissance Festival; Ivan Stutzman; Bailey Michael; Jamie Bosley; Jimmy McCue for his beautiful photo and Maryland Racing at Pimlico; Tonya Schoolcraft; The Western Maryland Scenic Railroad; Chesapeake Bay Maritime Museum; Keshawn Rhodes & Korey Mitchum; Keri & Ryan Strubin; Kory Bosley; David & Bryan Leonard; Cloe Strubin; Katie Eyler; and The Maryland Zoo in Baltimore.

The painting of *The Maryland Dove* (page D) is used with the permission of Historic St. Mary's City: P.O. Box 39, St. Mary's City, MD 20686, (240) 895-4967, www.stmaryscity.org.

Sleeping Bear Press™

310 North Main Street, Suite 300
Chelsea, MI 48118
www.sleepingbearpress.com

© 2004 Sleeping Bear Press is an imprint of Gale, a part of Cengage Learning.

Printed and bound in China.

10 9 8 7 6 5

Library of Congress Cataloging-in-Publication Data

Menendez, Shirley, 1937-
B is for blue crab : a Maryland alphabet / written by Shirley Menendez;
illustrated by Laura Stutzman.
p. cm.
ISBN 978-1-58536-160-1
1. Maryland—Juvenile literature. 2. English language—Alphabet—Juvenile
literature. I. Stutzman, Laura. II. Title.
F181.3.M46 2004
975.2—dc22
2004015444

To Albert
for his love and support

SHIRLEY

✤

To my children, Falon and Ivan, who are so precious to me.
And to the memory of their Uncle John, a child of the Chesapeake
who taught us all not to oversteer.

LAURA

Aa

This beautiful town has been Maryland's capital since 1695. It is the home of the Maryland State House, where our laws are made. It is the oldest state capitol building in the United States that is still in legislative use. The Governor's Mansion and the U.S. Naval Academy are located here.

The entire city of Annapolis has been declared a National Historical Landmark. It has more Colonial-era buildings than anywhere else in America. Annapolis was briefly the capital of the United States in 1783.

A is for Annapolis—
It is the government seat
and our state capital
where legislators meet.

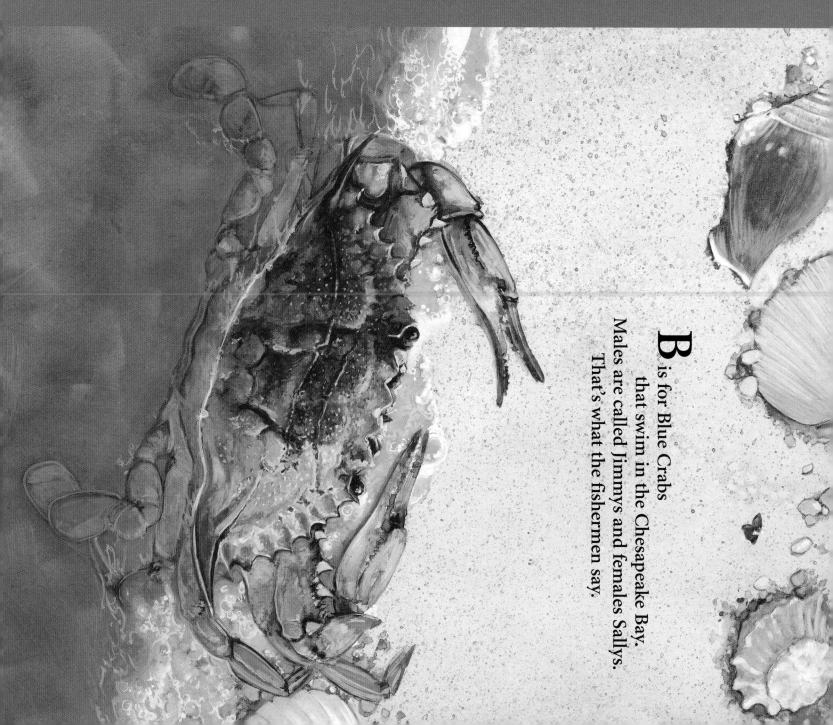

In 1989 the Maryland Blue Crab was designated the state crustacean. The scientific name of the blue crab, *Callinectes sapidus*, translates as "beautiful swimmer that is savory." Crab meat is prepared in many different ways, but Maryland is known for its crab cakes.

Fishermen call the male blue crab a "Jimmy." The young female blue crab is called "she-crab" or "Sally," while the adult female is called a "sook." One way to tell a male from a female crab is by the color of the claw tips. It looks like females paint their fingernails because they have bright red claw tips.

B also stands for Black-Eyed Susan, which has been the official state flower since 1918 when the Maryland General Assembly adopted it on April 18 of that year. It was chosen because its colorful orange petals with black center resemble the colors in the state flag. It grows in fields and on roadsides from May to August and can reach two to three feet in height.

B is for Blue Crabs
that swim in the Chesapeake Bay.
Males are called Jimmys and females Sallys.
That's what the fishermen say.

C is for the Chesapeake Bay
whose sandy shores are a delight.
Its waters are home to crabs and clams
while graceful birds are seen in flight.

The Chesapeake Bay is the largest estuary in the United States, stretching some 200 miles in length. Its mixture of salt and fresh waters makes it the perfect habitat for many types of creatures, including clams, oysters, striped bass, and crabs. A variety of wildlife lives along the Bay's shores, including the rare Delmarva fox squirrel and the endangered bald eagle.

The Chesapeake Bay Retriever was designated the official state dog in 1964. They are excellent hunters and swimmers and are used in duck hunting to retrieve ducks for their owner. Plunging into freezing water to retrieve the fallen ducks and geese requires skill and stamina, and these dogs are able to excel in this sport.

The *Ark* and the *Dove* left England in the fall of 1633 with over 200 colonists aboard. The two ships became separated in a fierce storm and it was feared that the *Dove* was lost, since it was a smaller ship. However, the *Dove* had gone ashore to wait out the storm and was able to reunite with the *Ark* at Barbados. After a brief stop in Virginia, the ships arrived at St. Clement's Island in St. Mary's County in March of 1634.

The *Ark* and the *Dove* carried both Catholics and Protestants to Maryland. They established the state as a religious sanctuary where people could worship as they pleased.

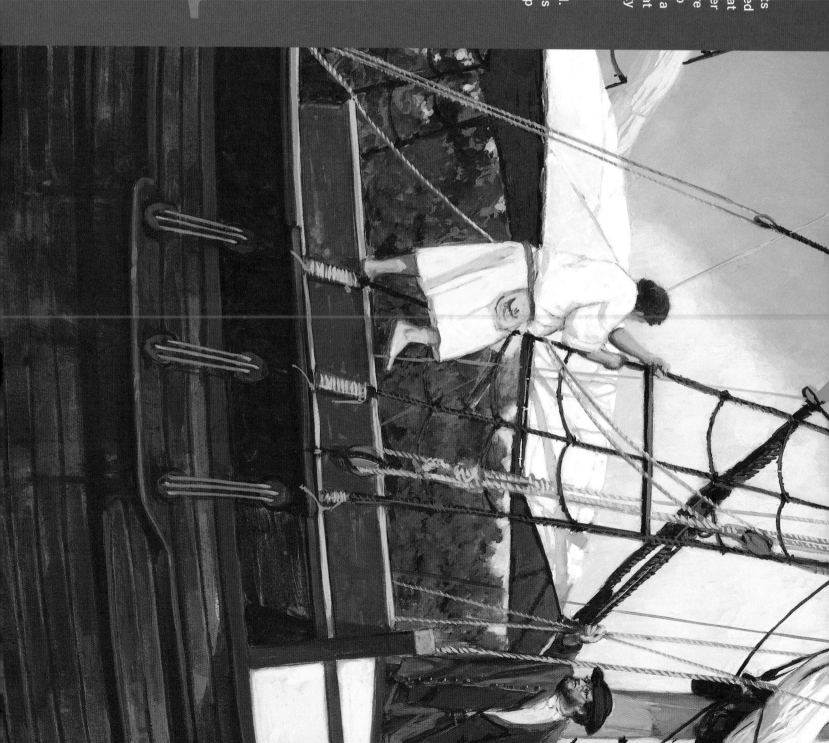

The *Ark* and the *Dove* were the famous ships that brought settlers to Maryland's shore. The *Dove*, which begins with the letter D, arrived along with the *Ark* in 1634.

E is for the Eastern Shore.
A place where you can play
on the shores of the Atlantic
or watch sailboats on the Bay.

The Eastern Shore is the name for the counties between the Chesapeake Bay and the Atlantic Ocean. This area was one of the earliest settled regions in the United States. The Nanticoke and Choptank Indian tribes lived here.

The small towns on the Eastern Shore are home to boat builders, sailors, fishermen, and sportsmen. Also, many crafters and artisans live in this area. One of the Eastern Shore towns, Ocean City, is a major attraction for those who enjoy the beach.

The famed, wild Chincoteague ponies can be seen on Assateague Island National Seashore. These shaggy, sturdy ponies are smaller than horses and are well adapted to the harsh seashore environment. They are believed to be descendants of horses that grazed on the island as early as the seventeeth century.

Fort Frederick begins with the letter F.
It was built with a strong stone wall.
During the French and Indian War
it provided protection for all.

Fort Frederick State Park is the site of the largest and best-preserved architectural example of an eighteenth-century frontier fort. Work was begun on Fort Frederick in 1756 at the beginning of the French and Indian War in order to protect the English settlers from the French and their Native American allies. It took almost two years to complete. The fort was unique because of its large size and its strong stone wall. Most other forts of the period were built of wood and earth. No military action occurred at Fort Frederick during the war, but it did serve as an important staging area and supply base. Also, many settlers fled to the fort for protection.

Fort Frederick State Park is located in the Cumberland Valley, near Big Pool, about 18 miles west of Hagerstown. Development of the park began in the 1920s, making it one of Maryland's first state parks. The park sponsors many historic events and reenactments throughout the year.

F f

Visit historic Glen Echo Park
which begins with the letter G.
Take a carousel ride on an antique horse
and find interesting things to do and see.

GE

Glen Echo Park is a famous amusement park that began in 1891 and is now run by the National Park Service. It provides a rich arts education program, sponsoring concerts, workshops, and festivals. An artist-in-residency program allows the public to see artists at work.

A special feature of the park is an antique hand-carved, hand-painted Dentzel carousel which is a delight to ride. Dentzel, a young German immigrant to the United States, built it in 1921. It is known as a "menagerie carousel" because of the variety of its animals. There are horses, rabbits, ostriches, a giraffe, deer, lion, and tiger. It also features two circus chariots. The carousel has recently been completely refurbished so its original beauty has been restored.

H

H stands for Historic battles, where brave soldiers led the fight during the American Civil War for what they believed was right.

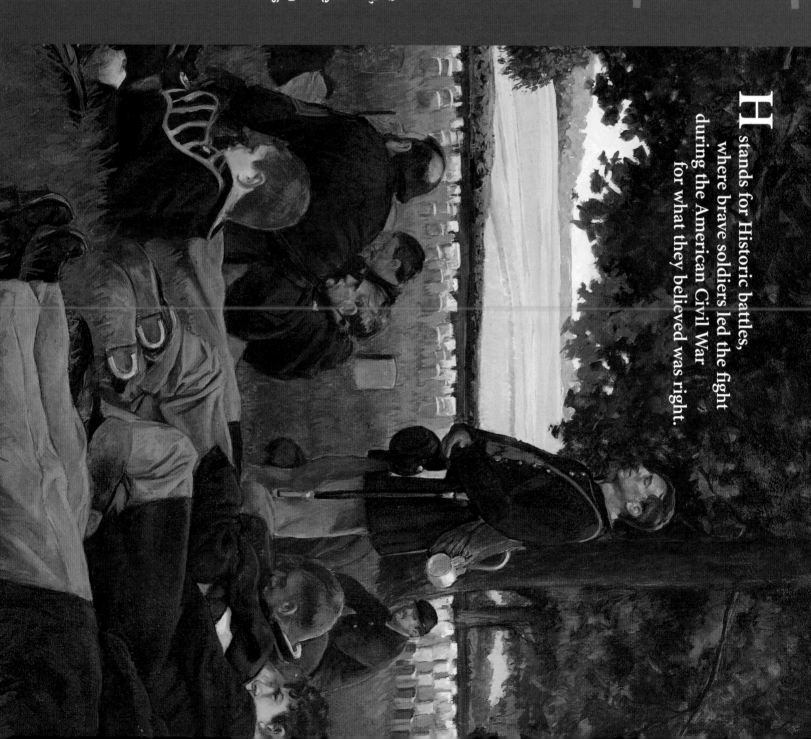

During the Civil War there were several battles fought in Maryland between the Northern and Southern armies. Antietam, in the Washington County town of Sharpsburg, was the site of the single bloodiest day in the Civil War. It was here in September 1862 that Robert E. Lee made an attempt to move into the North and faced a large Union army. Casualties were heavy on both sides. This battle led to President Lincoln's issuance of the Emancipation Proclamation to free the slaves.

The battle of Monocacy, which took place in Frederick, Maryland, in July 1864, is known as the "Battle That Saved Washington." The time spent in this battle cost the Confederate army a day's delay in marching on the federal capital. This delay allowed time for reinforcements to arrive, and Washington was saved.

You can visit the famous National Aquarium at the Inner Harbor, which begins with **I.** See animals, birds, reptiles, and fish, and watch the sharks as they swim by.

The harbor basin in Baltimore was run-down, with rotting wharves and abandoned warehouses until construction began on the Inner Harbor in the 1970s. Today the Inner Harbor contains many shops and eateries and is home to notable landmarks and attractions.

The National Aquarium is an Inner Harbor landmark and is one of the country's best aquariums. There are over 560 species of animals. You can see amphibians, birds, fish, mammals, and reptiles. The dolphin show is always exciting to watch. The aquarium also features an Amazon River Forest that has a variety of wildlife, from piranhas and giant turtles to a 300-pound green anaconda. A Tropical Rain Forest has parrots and monkeys. And an Atlantic Coral Reef features hundreds of vividly colored tropical fish. In another exhibit, a tank with large sharks encircles the visitor. The National Aquarium is always a fascinating place to visit.

Ii

J.j.

This sport originated in the Middle Ages when knights rode at each other with lances to unseat their opponents. Today's sport is a test of horsemanship and skill. Riders gallop at full speed and spear rings of various sizes. Rings are hung from supports that are 30 yards apart, and the knight who has speared the most rings becomes the champion. Both men and women compete in jousting.

Jousting was declared our state sport by the General Assembly in 1962. Maryland was the first state to designate an official state sport.

Think of knights on horses and you come to the letter J, which stands for a sport called Jousting. It is the state sport of Maryland today.

Kk

Francis Scott Key was a Maryland-born lawyer who wrote the stirring words to our national anthem, "The Star-Spangled Banner." During the War of 1812, Key was asked to help secure the release of a doctor who was held by the British. The release was accomplished, but Key was detained on a British ship in Baltimore Harbor. It was there that he witnessed the bombardment of Fort McHenry.

At daybreak, when he saw the American flag still flying over the fort, he was inspired to write the poem that was to become the United States' national anthem. Congress officially adopted it as our anthem in 1931.

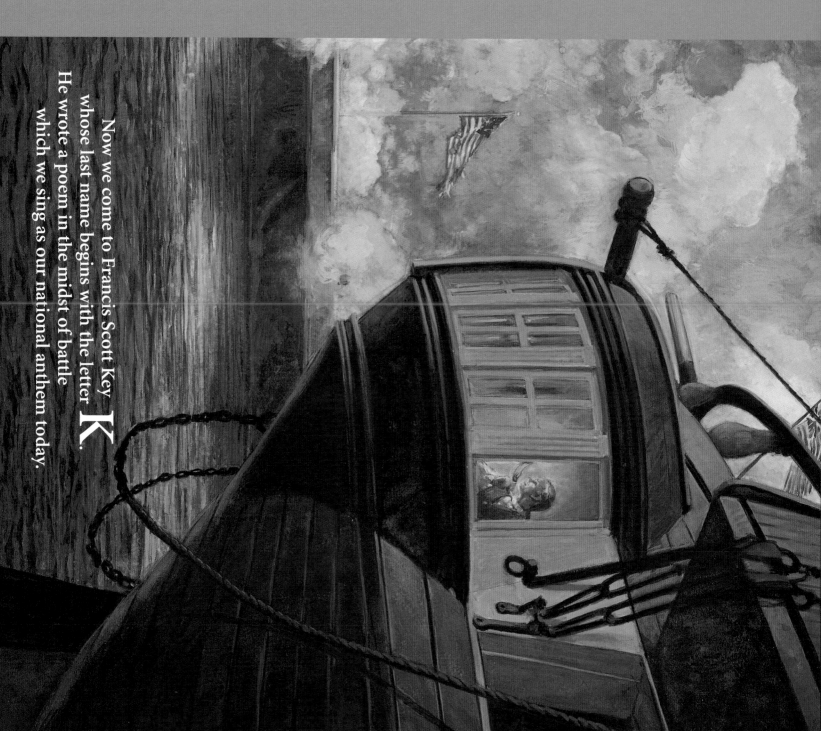

Now we come to Francis Scott Key whose last name begins with the letter K. He wrote a poem in the midst of battle which we sing as our national anthem today.

L is for the Lighthouse which guides ships through the night. It warns them with its signal and constant beams of light.

Lighthouses were built to guide ships at important or dangerous locations. They contain bright lights and foghorns or sirens to guide ships or warn of dangerous waters. There are over 20 lighthouses in Maryland, all on the Chesapeake Bay or its tributaries. Lighthouses were built in various shapes. The Concord Point and Drum Point lighthouses illustrate very different construction features.

Concord Point Light (illustrated here) in Havre de Grace was commissioned in 1827 to warn ships of currents and shoals where the Bay meets the Susquehanna River. It is a tower lighthouse, standing 39 feet high.

Drum Point Light was commissioned in 1883 to mark the entrance of the Patuxent River from the Chesapeake Bay. After restoration due to vandalism, it was moved to its current location at the Calvert Marine Museum in Solomons. It is one of the old screwpile, cottage-style lighthouses, a two-story, hexagon-shaped structure.

M

The letter **M** stands for Muddy Creek Falls which is a wondrous sight, where water flows over age-old rocks from an enormous height.

Muddy Creek Falls is our state's highest free-falling waterfall. The approximate height is between 54 and 63 feet. It falls over rocks that are millions of years old. It is located nine miles north of Oakland in Swallow Falls State Park in Garrett County.

Muddy Creek begins its journey in what is called the Cranesville Sub-Arctic Swamp, which is actually a high mountain bog. It is a remnant from the ice age and is located in a "frost pocket" where the surrounding hills capture moisture and cold air that creates a habitat normally found in the arctic regions. There are many rare species of plants and animals that live in the region. In 1965 it was designated a National Natural Landmark by the National Park Service.

The highest mountain in the state is located in Garrett County. The mountain is called Backbone and rises to 3,360 feet. Also, the state's largest lake can be found here. Deep Creek Lake is 12 miles long, with a beautiful shoreline.

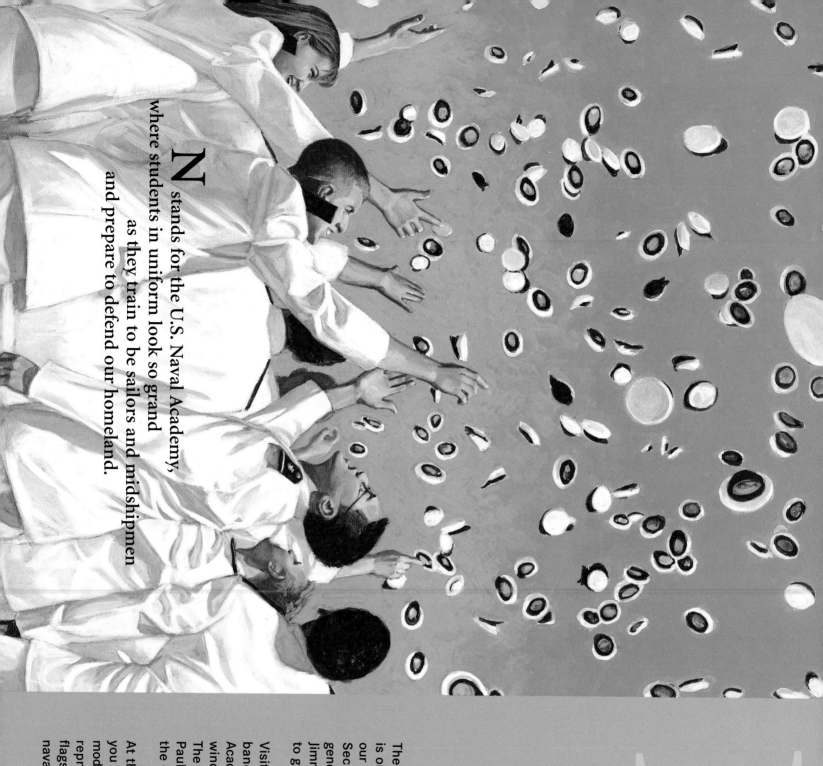

N stands for the U.S. Naval Academy, where students in uniform look so grand as they train to be sailors and midshipmen and prepare to defend our homeland.

The U.S. Naval Academy in Annapolis is one of the four service academies for our armed forces. Founded in 1845 by the Secretary of the Navy, it has produced generations of naval and marine officers. Jimmy Carter was the only U.S. president to graduate from the Naval Academy.

Visitors to the campus can enjoy the band and dress parade. The Naval Academy Chapel, with its beautiful Tiffany windows, is the site of many weddings. The Revolutionary War naval hero John Paul Jones is buried in the basement of the chapel.

At the U.S. Naval Academy Museum you can see a fascinating exhibit of model ships. There are also many items representing naval history, including flags, uniforms, medals, weapons, and naval documents.

A special bird brings us to O—
The Oriole's colors are bright.
With a black hood and breast of orange,
he is a beautiful sight.

The oriole gets its name from the Latin *oriolus*, meaning golden. The oriole's song is a clear flute-like whistle. The female builds a hanging nest that is superior to any other bird nest for its warmth and security. In 1882 the Maryland Legislature passed a law protecting the oriole. The Baltimore oriole was named the state bird in 1947. The Baltimore oriole's colors match those of the coat of arms of Lord Baltimore and was named for him.

The design of the Maryland state flag is also taken from the coats of arms of Lord Baltimore's family. The King of England granted the charter for the province of Maryland to Lord Baltimore. The flag is divided into four quarters. The black and gold quarters are the arms of his father's family, the Calverts. The red and white quarters are those of his mother's family, the Crosslands. Maryland's state flag was adopted in 1904.

Horse racing has long been a popular sport. The Preakness Stakes takes place every May at the Pimlico Race Course in Baltimore. The Preakness is the second step in horse racing's Triple Crown. The race is named for a winning horse called Preakness.

There is a long-standing tradition at the end of the race. A painter climbs a ladder to a five-foot-wide aluminum weather vane that is in the shape of a horse and rider. The colors of the winning owner's silks on the jockey and horse are painted on the weather vane.

Pp

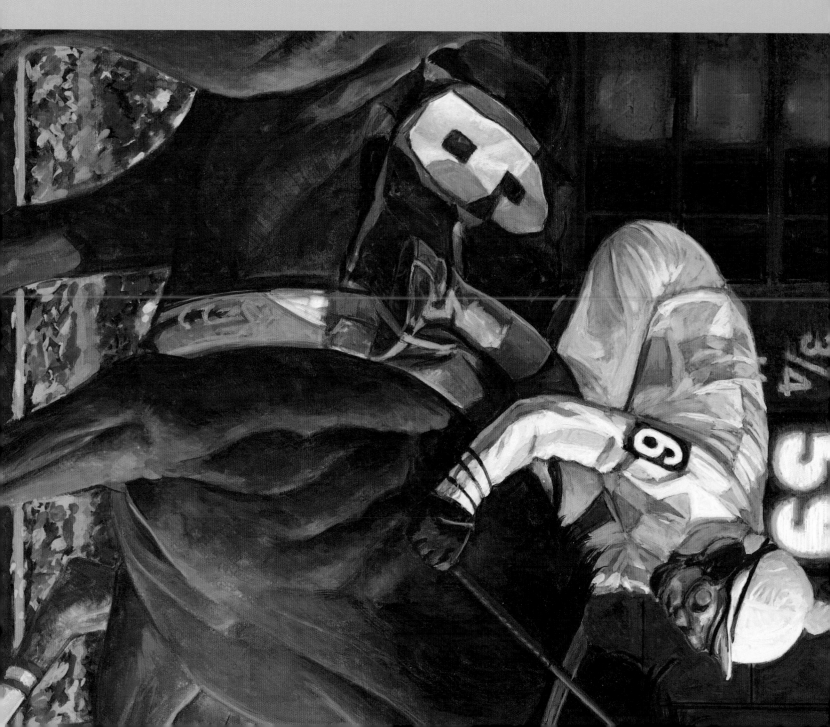

P is for the Preakness.
Jockeys and horses look so fine.
Excitement builds and the crowd cheers
as they race to the finish line.

Q stands for Queen Henrietta Maria, a Queen of England so grand that a colony was named for her and it became Maryland.

Henrietta Maria was in her teens when she was chosen to be the bride of England's King Charles I.

Although it was an arranged marriage, King Charles thought highly of this beautiful, intelligent young woman. When he granted the territory to Lord Baltimore, and they were searching for a name, the King suggested that the colony could be called Terra Mariae in honor of his Queen, and Lord Baltimore agreed. The charter was written in Latin and *Terra Mariae* is Latin for "Land of Mary." The name became Mary's Land or Maryland.

The letter **R** brings us to Railroads.

Trains are a faster way to go
than traveling on roads and ships
so Maryland built the B&O.

On August 4, 1828, Charles Carroll laid the cornerstone for the first railroad in America. The Baltimore and Ohio railroad extended 13 miles from Baltimore to Ellicott Mills. One of the first trains was a steam locomotive. By 1852 the B&O became America's longest railroad, reaching 379 miles to the Ohio Valley.

A B&O Museum now stands on the site of the first railroad station. It features vintage locomotives and railroad artifacts. Visitors can play conductor and engineer on the engines.

S is for the Skipjack, which gracefully sails away to pull the dredge for oysters on the Chesapeake Bay.

The skipjack is the last working boat under sail in North America. It got its name from the fish that playfully skip on the water's surface. The skipjack was developed in the 1890s to replace the larger and more expensive "bugeye" boat. It is vital to the state's fishing industry, since watermen are required by law to use sailboats rather than motorboats to dredge oysters from the bay. The skipjack was named a state symbol in 1985.

S also stands for Sideling Hill. Located approximately six miles west of Hancock in Washington County, it is one of the best rock exposures in the northeastern United States. Highway construction through the mountain exposed almost 850 vertical feet of rock that was formed nearly 350 million years ago. During the winter months a beautiful ice cascade can be seen as the water flowing over the rocks freezes into icicles.

S s

Tt

T is for Harriet Tubman, a hero in her time. She led black slaves to freedom on the Underground Railroad line.

Harriet Ross Tubman was born into slavery on a plantation in Dorchester County around 1820. When her master died in 1847, she fled to the North and freedom. She decided to become a conductor on the Underground Railroad and help other slaves escape. This was dangerous work and she often used disguises and changed her route so that she would not be caught. She personally escorted about 300 slaves to the North, including her own family, and came to be known as the "Moses of her people."

When the Civil War began, Tubman served as a nurse, scout, and spy for the Union army. After the war she worked tirelessly for women's rights and justice for all. In 1978 the U.S. Postal Service released a stamp honoring Harriet Tubman.

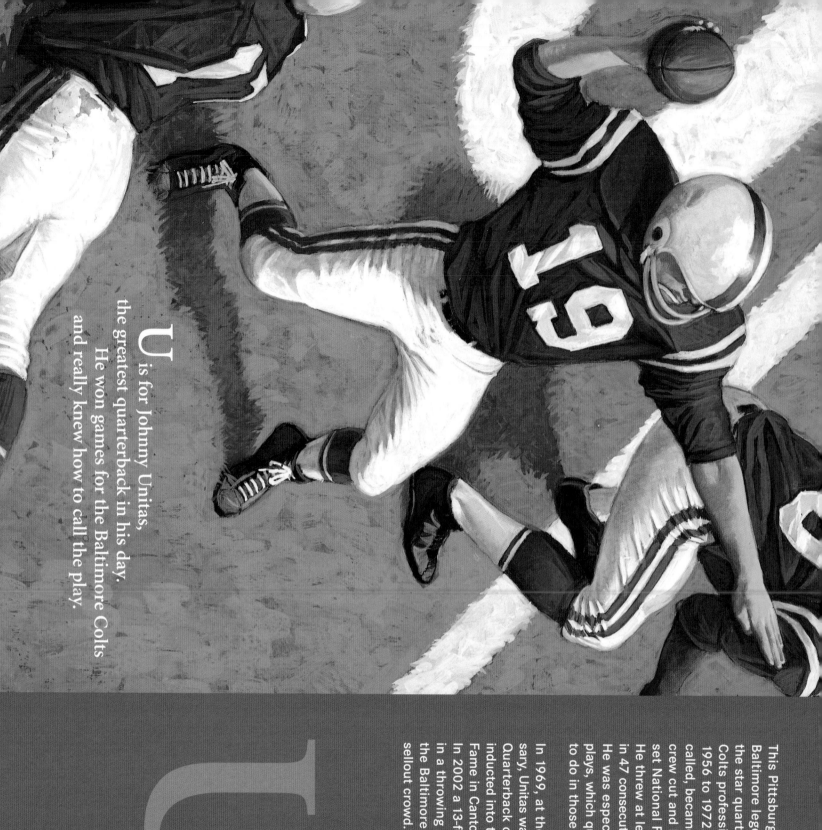

U is for Johnny Unitas,
the greatest quarterback in his day.
He won games for the Baltimore Colts
and really knew how to call the play.

U
u

This Pittsburgh native became a Baltimore legend. Johnny Unitas was the star quarterback for the Baltimore Colts professional football team from 1956 to 1972. Johnny U, as he was called, became known for his signature crew cut and black high-top shoes. He set National Football League records. He threw at least one touchdown pass in 47 consecutive regular-season games. He was especially good at calling the plays, which quarterbacks were allowed to do in those days.

In 1969, at the NFL's 50th anniversary, Unitas was named the "Greatest Quarterback of All-Time." He was inducted into the Pro Football Hall of Fame in Canton, Ohio, 10 years later. In 2002 a 13-foot statue of Johnny U in a throwing pose was unveiled at the Baltimore Ravens stadium to a sellout crowd.

Vv

The American Visionary Art Museum opened in Baltimore's Inner Harbor in 1996. It is the first museum in the country devoted to works by self-taught artists. These works are called "outsider" or "visionary art."

The museum includes an educational center, seven galleries to display works of art, and a sculpture barn. It even has a café serving "edible art," which is food shaped like art.

Maryland also has several other notable museums including the Walters Art Gallery in Baltimore and the Baltimore Museum of Art. The Ward Museum of Wildfowl Art in Salisbury has one of the world's finest collections of antique duck decoys.

V is for the Visionary Art Museum, where untrained artists like you and me can display their works of art for all who want to come and see.

Ww

Watermen are independent fishermen who make their living fishing for crabs, clams, and oysters on the Chesapeake Bay. The seafood industry was once a thriving business in Maryland and watermen could make a good living. Today pollution of the waters has caused a decline in the number of clams, crabs, and oysters that can be harvested. Many watermen have had to find other ways to make a living, but some still struggle to maintain their way of life.

In recognition of the contributions of the watermen, the state authorized a Maryland Watermen's Monument to be located in Kent Narrows in Queen Anne's County.

W stands for Watermen—
Fishing is their trade.
They dredge for oysters in the Bay.
That's how their living is made.

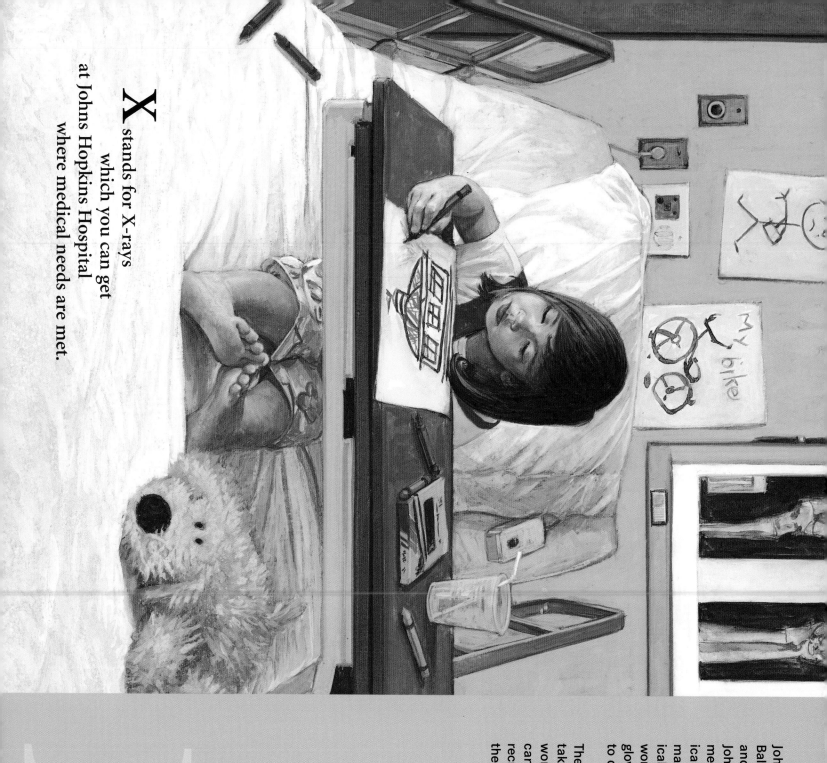

X stands for X-rays
which you can get
at Johns Hopkins Hospital
where medical needs are met.

Johns Hopkins medical institution in Baltimore has one of the most respected and advanced medical care systems. Johns Hopkins remains a world leader in medical teaching, patient care, and medical discovery. Its achievements include many firsts. It was the first major medical school in the United States to admit women. It was also the first to use rubber gloves during surgery. And it was the first to develop CPR and renal dialysis.

The Johns Hopkins Children's Center has taken care of children from around the world. In addition to excellent medical care, the hospital provides a variety of recreational activities to help children and their families cope with hospitalization.

Y stands for Camden Yards
where the Baltimore Orioles play.
    Although the park is new,
it looks like the olden days.

Oriole Park at Camden Yards is a state-of-the-art ballpark for the Baltimore Orioles. It took 33 months to complete and opened on April 6, 1992. Although it is up-to-date in all of its features, the park was built to resemble the early twentieth-century baseball fields. It is faced with brick to present a traditional appearance. It has several special features. Each aisle seat features an 1890s Orioles logo. In left center field there are unique double-decked bullpens. A bronze statue honors the legendary Babe Ruth at the Eutaw Street entrance to Oriole Park. His birthplace is located nearby.

Another famous ballplayer at the park was Calvin Edwin Ripken Jr., known as Cal. He played shortstop and later third base for the Baltimore Orioles. He set a baseball record by playing in more consecutive games (2,632) than any other player in history. It was on September 6, 1995, that Ripken passed the record set in 1939 by the beloved Lou Gehrig of the New York Yankees.

Zoo begins with the letter Z.
Animals who live at The Maryland Zoo
include elephants, monkeys, tigers, and lions,
and you can see the polar bears, too.

Zoos are always a fun place to learn about the animal kingdom. Over 2,000 animals live at The Maryland Zoo in Baltimore. Magnet and Alaska are the zoo's famous polar bears. The zoo also offers exhibits where you can take a safari through Africa or explore a path through a wilderness.

Another zoo in Maryland, the Salisbury Zoo, opened in 1954. It got its start when some animals were placed on permanent exhibit in the City Park. This zoo features almost 500 species of animals that are native to North, Central, and South America.

A Bay Full of Facts

1. What are the colors in the Maryland state flag?

2. Who composed the words to our national anthem?

3. What is the name of the baseball field where the Orioles play?

4. Name the state sport of Maryland.

5. Where can you ride on an antique carousel?

6. When is the Preakness Stakes run?

7. What is the state bird?

8. Name the ships that brought settlers to Maryland's shores.

9. Which baseball star set a record by playing in more consecutive games than any other player?

10. What is the name of the sailboat that is used to dredge for oysters on the Chesapeake Bay?

11. What is the state flower?

12. Where can you find the tomb of John Paul Jones?

13. What city is the capital of Maryland?

14. Where can you find the blue crab?

15. Which Colts football player was called the "Greatest Quarterback of All-Time"?

Answers

1. Red, white, black, and gold
2. Francis Scott Key
3. Oriole Park at Camden Yards
4. Jousting
5. Glen Echo Park
6. May
7. Baltimore oriole
8. *Ark* and *Dove*

9. Cal Ripken Jr.
10. Skipjack
11. Black-eyed Susan
12. In the chapel at the U.S. Naval Academy
13. Annapolis
14. Chesapeake Bay
15. Johnny Unitas

Shirley C. Menendez

Shirley C. Menendez grew up in Staunton, Virginia, and graduated from Mary Baldwin College. She earned a master's degree in library science from Drexel University. She fell in love with picture books when she conducted story hours as a librarian. Before joining the administrative staff of Georgetown University she was a librarian in the Prince George's County Memorial Library System in Maryland and the Westchester Library System in New York.

Shirley lives in North Potomac, Maryland, with her husband Albert, who is also a writer. They have written several books together.

Laura Stutzman

Laura Stutzman graduated from the Art Institute of Pittsburgh and later formed a studio called Eloqui in 1984 with her partner and husband Mark. She has created imagery for books and magazines, corporations, nonprofit organizations, and privately commissioned portraits. Her studio is in her home in Mountain Lake Park, Maryland, which, a century ago, was a Chautauqua, a "summer camp" for adults dedicated to teaching an appreciation for the arts and humanities.

Thanks to the sponsorship of the Sprenger-Lang Foundation, Laura teaches painting at an annual, week-long workshop to kids grades 8 through 12 who are serious about art. Laura shares her home with Mark and her son Ivan, a tiny dog, two cats, and a ferret. Her daughter Falon is a college student. You can see Laura's work at www.eloqui.com.